Canada 123

illustrated by
Per-Henrik Gürth

written by
Kim Bellefontaine

Kids Can Press

Printed especially for The Learning Partnership's Welcome to Kindergarten™ program.

THE LEARNING PARTNERSHIP
Champions of Public Education Across Canada

www.thelearningpartnership.ca

One maple leaf blowing in the wind.

Two polar bears playing in the snow.

Three totem poles
standing tall on the West Coast.

Four skiers swooshing down the slopes.

5

Five farmers
harvesting their crop.

6 Six canoes
gliding across the lake.

Seven hockey players skating on a pond.

8

Eight wolves
howling at the moon.

Nine fishing boats bobbing on the waves.

Ten tulips blooming on Parliament Hill.

More things to count!

1

2

3

4

5

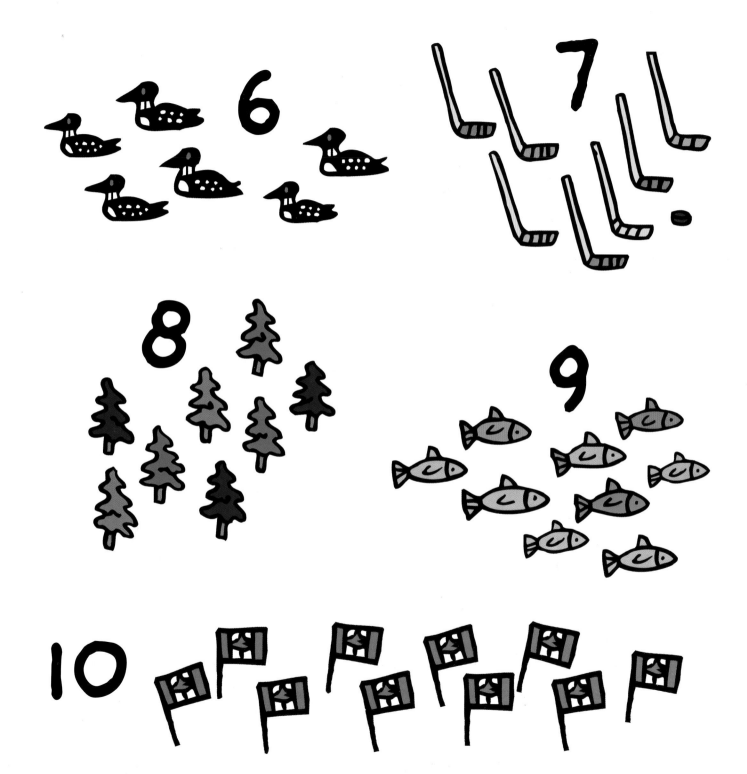

To our son, Benjamin — K.B. and P-H.G.

Text © 2006 Kim Bellefontaine
Illustrations © 2006 Per-Henrik Gürth

This edition printed especially for The Learning Partnership's
Welcome to Kindergarten™ program.

ISBN 978-1-55453-421-0 (pbk.)

CM PA 08 0 9 8 7 6 5 4 3 2

Kids Can Press acknowledges the financial support of the
Government of Ontario, through the Ontario Media Development
Corporation's Ontario Book Initiative; the Ontario Arts Council; the
Canada Council for the Arts; and the Government of Canada,
through the BPIDP, for our publishing activity.

Published in Canada by
Kids Can Press Ltd.
29 Birch Avenue
Toronto, ON M4V 1E2

Published in the U.S. by
Kids Can Press Ltd.
2250 Military Road
Tonawanda, NY 14150

www.kidscanpress.com

The artwork in this book was rendered in Adobe Illustrator.
The text is set in Providence-Sans Bold.

Edited by Yvette Ghione
Designed by Per-Henrik Gürth and Céleste Gagnon
Printed and bound in China

CM 06 0 9 8 7 6 5 4 3 2

Library and Archives Canada Cataloguing in Publication

Gürth, Per-Henrik
        Canada 123 / illustrated by Per-Henrik Gürth ; written by Kim
Bellefontaine.

ISBN 978-1-55337-897-6

1. Counting — Juvenile literature. 2. Canada — Miscellanea — Juvenile literature.
I. Bellefontaine, Kim (Kim Anne) II. Title. III. Title: Canada one, two, three.

QA113.G87 2006   j513.2'11   C2005-902221-3

Kids Can Press is a ℓorus™ Entertainment company